Dyspraxia Decode

A Parent's Guide to Helping Your Child Thrive

By

Jagdish Prasad Yadav

Senior Occupational Therapist

Newbee Publication

Copyright © Newbee Publication 2024 All Rights Reserved

No part of this publication may be reproduced, stored in a retrieval system, or transmitted in any form or by any means—electronic, mechanical, photocopying, recording, or otherwise—without the prior written permission of the publisher.

Thank you for your purchase, scan the QR code for more publications.

Disclaimer

This self-help guide is intended as an educational resource for parents awaiting professional assessment of their children. It is not a substitute for clinical judgment or individual advice. The ideas expressed herein are not intended for diagnosing children and should not be taken as a comprehensive guide to all conditions or childhood issues, such as developmental delays, learning disorders, or childhood disorders. Parents are encouraged to exercise individual discretion at all times and consult relevant health professionals when needed.

The suggested activities are not substitutes for therapy. If there are significant gaps in your child's progress, please reach out to local therapists or other appropriate professionals. While we strive to ensure that the information provided is accurate and up to date, it is not a replacement for professional advice tailored to your specific situation. To the extent permitted by law, we assume no liability for the use of information in this publication, nor any third-party reports or websites referenced within.

Table of Content

Contents

Chapter 1:

Introduction: Understanding Dyspraxia/Developmental Coordination Disorder (DCD)........................... 6

Chapter 1: Understanding Dyspraxia................... 9

    Conclusion....................................... 14

Chapter 2: Coming to Terms with the Diagnosis... 15

    EmbracingtheJourney   20

Chapter 3: Building a Support Network............... 21

Chapter 4: Strategies for Daily Living............. 27

    EncouragementandSupport   32

Chapter 5: Supporting Motor Skills Development.. 32

    Task-OrientedApproaches   37

    EncouragementandPatience   38

Chapter 6: Enhancing Learning and Academic Performance.. 39

    IncorporatingTechnologyin Learning   44

    EncouragementandSupport   44

Chapter 7: Nurturing Social Skills and Emotional Well-Being... 45

    SupportingHolisticWell-Being   49

Chapter 8: Physical Activities and Sports.................. 50

    Promoting Inclusion in Sports   54

Chapter 9: Planning for the Future........................... 55

    Empowering the Journey Ahead......................... 60

Chapter 10: Self-Care for Parents................................ 61

    Taking Care of Yourself Benefits Everyone......... 65

Recap of Key Points 66

Appendices.. 67

Looking Ahead.. 69

This book structure provides a comprehensive guide for parents, covering the journey from initial concerns through diagnosis and ongoing support. It addresses practical strategies, emotional aspects, and long-term planning, making it a valuable resource for parents at various stages of their child's dyspraxia journey

Introduction: Understanding Dyspraxia/Developmental Coordination Disorder (DCD)

Dyspraxia, also known as Developmental Coordination Disorder (DCD), is a neurodevelopmental condition that affects motor coordination, planning, and execution of movements. It impacts individuals differently and is often present alongside other challenges such as difficulties in learning, attention, or social interaction. Despite these hurdles, individuals with dyspraxia possess unique strengths and potential that, when nurtured, allow them to thrive.

What is Dyspraxia/DCD?

Dyspraxia is characterized by difficulties in:

- Motor Coordination: Challenges with fine and gross motor skills, making tasks like writing, tying shoelaces, or riding a bike more difficult.
- Motor Planning: Struggling to sequence and organize movements, which affects daily activities such as dressing or participating in sports.
- Sensory Processing: Difficulties integrating sensory information can lead to clumsiness or trouble navigating environments.

How Common is Dyspraxia?

- It affects approximately 5–6% of school-aged children, with boys diagnosed more often than girls.

- Although it is commonly identified in childhood, dyspraxia persists into adulthood for many individuals, affecting their daily lives and career choices.

Understanding the Challenges

While dyspraxia does not affect intelligence, it can influence:

- Academic Performance: Handwriting, organization, and time management are common areas of difficulty.
- Daily Living Skills: Tasks such as eating, dressing, and personal care may require extra time and effort.
- Social Interaction: Motor challenges can affect participation in group activities, potentially impacting friendships and self-esteem.

Strengths of Individuals with Dyspraxia

Despite these challenges, individuals with dyspraxia often exhibit remarkable strengths, including:

- Creativity and originality in problem-solving.
- Empathy and resilience in the face of adversity.
- Determination to overcome obstacles and achieve their goals.

The Purpose of This Book

This guide aims to provide parents, caregivers, and educators with:

- Practical Strategies: Actionable steps to support motor skills, academic performance, and emotional well-being.
- Evidence-Based Insights: The latest research on dyspraxia, including neuroimaging findings and intervention techniques.
- Emotional Support: Advice for parents navigating the challenges of raising a child with dyspraxia.
- Hope and Inspiration: Stories of success that highlight the potential of individuals with dyspraxia.

By understanding dyspraxia and learning effective ways to support individuals with this condition, we can empower them to navigate their unique journeys and reach their full potential. This book is not just about managing challenges—it's about celebrating strengths and unlocking opportunities for growth and achievement.

Chapter 1: Understanding Dyspraxia

Dyspraxia, or Developmental Coordination Disorder (DCD), is a complex and often misunderstood condition. In this chapter, we'll explore its definition, key characteristics, symptoms, differences from other conditions, and the factors contributing to its prevalence and causes.

Definition and Characteristics of Dyspraxia

Dyspraxia is a neurodevelopmental condition that affects the ability to plan, coordinate, and execute movements. It is recognized by the Diagnostic and Statistical Manual of

Mental Disorders (DSM-5) under the category of Developmental Coordination Disorder (DCD).

Key Characteristics:

- **Motor Coordination Difficulties**: Challenges with both fine motor skills (e.g., writing, using scissors) and gross motor skills (e.g., running, jumping).
- **Motor Planning Issues**: Difficulty sequencing and organizing movements required for daily tasks.
- **Developmental Delays**: Milestones such as crawling, walking, or speaking may be achieved later than peers.
- **Impact on Daily Living**: Struggles with dressing, eating, and other self-care activities.
- **Normal Intelligence**: While dyspraxia affects motor skills, cognitive abilities are typically unaffected, though learning can be impacted.

Common Symptoms and Challenges

Dyspraxia manifests differently depending on age, and the symptoms can range from mild to severe. Below are some common indicators:

Early Childhood (0–5 years):

- Delayed milestones, such as rolling over, crawling, or walking.
- Difficulty gripping objects or using utensils.
- Poor balance and frequent falling.
- Challenges with speech clarity or learning to speak.

School-Age Children (6–12 years):

- Handwriting difficulties, such as illegibility or slow writing speed.
- Problems with sports, particularly those requiring coordination, like catching or kicking a ball.
- Difficulty tying shoelaces, using buttons, or handling zippers.
- Organizational and time-management challenges, affecting schoolwork and routines.
- Frustration or avoidance of physical activities due to repeated failures.

Adolescents and Adults:

- Persistent clumsiness and awkward movements.
- Challenges with driving or learning new motor skills.
- Social difficulties stemming from poor coordination in group activities.
- Fatigue caused by the extra effort required for everyday tasks.

Emotional and Social Impact:

- Low self-esteem or self-confidence due to frequent failures in motor-related tasks.
- Anxiety or frustration in social or academic settings.
- Avoidance of activities that highlight motor difficulties.

Differences Between Dyspraxia and Other Conditions

Dyspraxia shares overlapping features with other conditions, making accurate diagnosis essential. Understanding these distinctions can help parents and professionals better support individuals.

Dyspraxia vs. ADHD:

- ADHD primarily affects attention and impulse control, whereas dyspraxia focuses on motor coordination.
- Both conditions can involve organizational challenges, but for different reasons.

Dyspraxia vs. Autism Spectrum Disorder (ASD):

- ASD is characterized by difficulties in social communication and restricted interests, which are not primary features of dyspraxia.
- Dyspraxia-related motor issues may overlap with motor difficulties seen in ASD.

Dyspraxia vs. Dyslexia:

- Dyslexia primarily affects reading, writing, and language processing.
- Dyspraxia affects motor coordination, though both conditions can impact handwriting.

Dyspraxia vs. Sensory Processing Disorder (SPD):

- SPD focuses on how sensory information is processed, while dyspraxia involves motor planning and execution.
- Sensory challenges can co-occur with dyspraxia but are not its defining feature.

Dyspraxia vs. Cerebral Palsy:

- Cerebral palsy results from brain damage, typically at or before birth, leading to more severe motor impairments.
- Dyspraxia is a developmental disorder without clear evidence of brain injury.

Prevalence and Causes

Dyspraxia is more common than often recognized and affects individuals across all demographics.

Prevalence:

- Approximately 5–6% of school-aged children are diagnosed with dyspraxia.
- The condition is more frequently identified in males, with a male-to-female ratio ranging from 2:1 to 7:1. However, it may be underdiagnosed in females.

Causes: The exact causes of dyspraxia are not fully understood, but research suggests a combination of genetic and environmental factors.

- **Genetic Predisposition**: Families with a history of dyspraxia or related neurodevelopmental disorders may have an increased likelihood of occurrence.
- **Prenatal Influences**: Complications during pregnancy, such as low birth weight or premature delivery, are associated with higher risk.
- **Neurological Differences**: Research using neuroimaging indicates structural and functional differences in areas of the brain responsible for motor control and planning.
- **Environmental Factors**: Limited opportunities for physical activity and motor skill practice during early childhood may exacerbate symptoms but are not direct causes.

Conclusion

The process of diagnosing dyspraxia is comprehensive and often involves a team of professionals working together to understand a child's unique challenges and strengths. Recognizing the signs early and seeking appropriate help can lead to timely interventions that significantly improve outcomes for children with dyspraxia. By understanding the diagnostic process, parents and caregivers can navigate this journey with confidence, ensuring that their child receives the support they need to thrive.

Chapter 2: Coming to Terms with the Diagnosis

Receiving a dyspraxia diagnosis can be a deeply emotional experience for both parents and children. While it may bring clarity and answers, it also marks the beginning of a journey filled with adjustments, advocacy, and support. This chapter explores the emotional impact of the diagnosis, strategies for acceptance, ways to explain dyspraxia to your child, and addressing siblings' concerns.

Emotional Impact on Parents and Children

A diagnosis of dyspraxia can evoke a range of emotions for families, from relief to worry. Understanding these feelings is the first step toward navigating them effectively.

- **For Parents:**
    - Relief and Validation: The diagnosis may confirm what you've long suspected and provide a roadmap for next steps.
    - Guilt or Self-Doubt: Parents may wonder if they could have done something differently. Remember, dyspraxia is a neurodevelopmental condition, not caused by parenting choices.
    - Anxiety About the Future: Concerns about your child's academic success, social interactions, and independence are natural.
    - Empowerment: The diagnosis also opens doors to resources, support, and strategies to help your child thrive.
- **For Children:**
    - Confusion: Younger children may not fully understand the implications of the diagnosis.
    - Frustration: They may feel different from their peers or struggle with tasks others find easy.
    - Relief: Older children might feel relieved to have an explanation for their challenges.
    - Empowerment: With proper support, children can embrace their strengths and develop self-confidence.

Strategies for Accepting and Embracing the Diagnosis

Acceptance is an ongoing process that involves understanding, reframing, and adapting to new realities. Here's how parents can navigate this journey:

- **Educate Yourself:**
    - Learn about dyspraxia through books, webinars, and trusted online resources.
    - Familiarize yourself with strategies to support your child's development.
- **Shift Your Perspective:**
    - Focus on your child's strengths and celebrate their unique abilities.
    - Remember that challenges present opportunities for growth and resilience.
- **Build a Support System:**
    - Connect with other parents of children with dyspraxia through support groups or online communities.
    - Seek guidance from professionals, such as occupational therapists or counselors.
- **Practice Self-Compassion:**
    - Acknowledge your feelings without judgment.
    - Set realistic expectations for yourself and your family.
- **Celebrate Milestones:**
    - Recognize and celebrate small victories, from tying a shoelace to completing a school project.

- Use these achievements as motivation for future progress.

How to Explain Dyspraxia to Your Child

Helping your child understand their diagnosis can empower them to navigate their world with confidence. Tailor your approach to their age and comprehension level.

- **Use Simple Language:**
    - For younger children: "Your brain works in a special way, and sometimes it takes a little more practice to do certain things. That's okay!"
    - For older children: "Dyspraxia means your brain and body work a bit differently, but with some extra effort and the right help, you can do amazing things."
- **Highlight Strengths:**
    - Emphasize their talents and remind them that everyone has areas where they excel and areas where they need help.
    - Share stories of successful individuals with dyspraxia to inspire confidence.
- **Encourage Questions:**
    - Create a safe space for your child to ask questions about their diagnosis.
    - Be honest and reassuring, focusing on solutions and support.
- **Provide Tools for Self-Advocacy:**
    - Teach your child to explain dyspraxia in their own words.

- Help them understand how to ask for help when needed.

Addressing Siblings' Concerns and Questions

Siblings may have their own feelings and questions about the diagnosis. Open communication is key to fostering understanding and unity.

- **Acknowledge Their Feelings:**
  - Siblings may feel confused, jealous, or even overlooked. Validate their emotions without dismissing them.
  - Reassure them that their feelings are normal and important.
- **Explain Dyspraxia in Age-Appropriate Terms:**
  - Help siblings understand that dyspraxia is a condition that makes some things harder for their brother or sister.
  - Emphasize that it doesn't define their sibling's worth or potential.
- **Promote Inclusion:**
  - Encourage siblings to participate in activities and therapies that support their brother or sister.
  - Highlight the role they play in creating a positive and supportive family environment.
- **Address Concerns About Fairness:**
  - Explain that while their sibling may need extra help in some areas, each child is equally loved and supported.
  - Provide examples of ways they also receive unique attention.

- **Involve Siblings in Problem-Solving:**
    - Encourage siblings to suggest ideas for helping their brother or sister.
    - Celebrate their contributions to the family's journey.

Embracing the Journey

Coming to terms with a dyspraxia diagnosis is a journey of growth, adaptation, and advocacy. By addressing emotional responses, embracing the diagnosis, and fostering open communication, families can create a supportive environment where every member feels valued and empowered. This understanding lays the foundation for a stronger, more connected family unit.

Chapter 3: Building a Support Network

Building a robust support network is crucial for parents navigating the challenges of dyspraxia. This network can provide emotional support, practical assistance, and valuable resources to help your child thrive. In this chapter, we'll explore strategies for working with healthcare professionals, collaborating with educators, finding support groups and resources, and advocating for your child's needs.

Working with Healthcare Professionals

Healthcare professionals play a vital role in managing dyspraxia and supporting your child's development. Here's how to effectively collaborate with them:

- **Establish a Core Team**:
    - Pediatrician: Your primary point of contact for overall health and referrals.
    - Occupational Therapist: Focuses on improving fine motor skills and daily living activities.
    - Physiotherapist: Helps with gross motor skills and coordination.
    - Speech and Language Therapist: Addresses communication challenges, if present.
- **Maintain Open Communication**:
    - Keep a journal of your child's progress and challenges to share during appointments.
    - Prepare a list of questions or concerns ahead of consultations.
    - Don't hesitate to ask for clarification on medical terms or recommendations.
- **Follow Through on Recommendations**:
    - Implement suggested exercises or interventions at home consistently.
    - Provide feedback to healthcare professionals about what works and what doesn't.
- **Coordinate Care**:
    - Ensure all professionals involved in your child's care communicate with each other.

- Use tools like shared care plans or communication notebooks to streamline information sharing.

Collaborating with Educators

Teachers and school staff are key members of your child's support network. Here's how to establish a productive partnership:

- **Understand Your Rights**:
  - Familiarize yourself with special education laws and services in your area.
  - Know what accommodations your child is entitled to, such as Individualized Education Plans (IEPs) or 504 Plans.
- **Establish a Communication System**:
  - Set up regular meetings with teachers to discuss your child's progress.
  - Use tools like communication notebooks or weekly emails to stay updated.
- **Advocate for Classroom Support**:
  - Request seating arrangements that minimize distractions.
  - Encourage the use of assistive technology, such as text-to-speech software or adapted keyboards.
  - Suggest visual aids, task breakdowns, and movement breaks to help your child stay engaged.
- **Educate Educators**:
  - Provide teachers with resources or information about dyspraxia.

- Share strategies that work well at home to ensure consistency.

Finding Support Groups and Resources

Connecting with other parents and professionals who understand your journey can provide invaluable support:

- **Local Support Groups**:
    - Check community centers, hospitals, or parent advocacy organizations for local groups.
    - Attend meetings to share experiences and gain practical advice.
- **Online Communities**:
    - Join forums, social media groups, or virtual support networks focused on dyspraxia.
    - Participate in discussions to exchange tips and resources.
- **National Organizations**:
    - Reach out to dyspraxia-focused organizations for webinars, publications, and workshops.
    - Many organizations also provide directories of healthcare providers and services.
- **Educational Resources**:
    - Utilize books, articles, and videos to expand your understanding of dyspraxia.
    - Share these resources with family members or educators to foster a supportive environment.

Advocating for Your Child's Needs

Advocacy is a powerful tool to ensure your child gets the support they need. Here are strategies to become an effective advocate:

- **Educate Yourself**:
    - Learn about dyspraxia, special education laws, and available resources.
    - Stay updated on the latest research and interventions.
- **Document Everything**:
    - Keep records of meetings, assessments, and correspondence with schools or healthcare providers.
    - Use these records to track progress and support your advocacy efforts.
- **Build Positive Relationships**:
    - Approach interactions with educators and healthcare professionals as collaborative rather than confrontational.
    - Focus on solutions that prioritize your child's best interests.
- **Teach Self-Advocacy**:
    - As your child grows, involve them in discussions about their needs.
    - Encourage them to express their challenges and preferences in a safe environment.
- **Seek Support When Needed**:
    - Consider enlisting the help of an educational advocate if you face challenges in securing accommodations.

- Some organizations offer parent training programs to enhance advocacy skills.

Building a strong support network takes time and effort, but it's an essential foundation for your child's success. By working closely with healthcare professionals, collaborating with educators, connecting with support groups, and advocating effectively, you'll create an environment that empowers your child to reach their full potential.

Chapter 4: Strategies for Daily Living

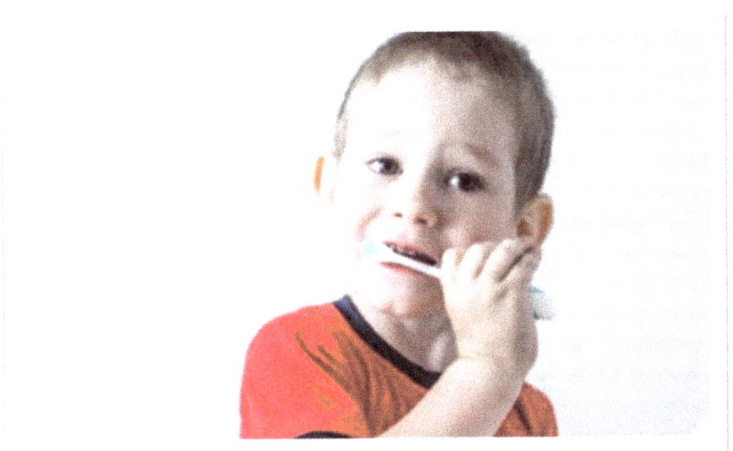

For children with dyspraxia, daily living tasks can present unique challenges. With the right strategies, these activities can become opportunities to build independence, confidence, and life skills. This chapter focuses on practical tips for dressing and personal care, eating and drinking, organization and time management, and establishing effective sleep routines.

Dressing and Personal Care

Dressing and grooming can be difficult for children with dyspraxia due to fine motor coordination and sequencing challenges. Here's how to make these tasks more manageable:

- **Simplify Clothing Choices**:
    - Opt for clothing with simple fastenings like Velcro or elastic waistbands.
    - Avoid items with small buttons, tight zippers, or tricky closures.
- **Organize Outfits**:
    - Lay out clothes the night before to minimize morning stress.
    - Use labeled bins or color-coded hangers for easy outfit selection.
- **Practice Dressing Techniques**:
    - Break down dressing into small, sequential steps (e.g., "First put on the shirt, then the pants").
    - Use visual guides or checklists to reinforce routines.
- **Adapt Clothing**:
    - Add zipper pulls, elastic shoelaces, or magnetic fasteners to make items easier to handle.
    - Choose slip-on shoes or footwear with Velcro straps.
- **Support Personal Care**:
    - Use electric toothbrushes or razors for ease and efficiency.
    - Install grab bars and non-slip mats in bathrooms to enhance safety.
    - Teach step-by-step grooming tasks with verbal prompts or visual aids.

Eating and Drinking

Mealtime challenges for children with dyspraxia often stem from hand-eye coordination or sensory sensitivities. Here are strategies to improve eating and drinking skills:

- **Introduce Adaptive Utensils**:
    - Use utensils with larger, ergonomic handles for easier grip.
    - Try weighted utensils or plates with suction bases to reduce spills.
- **Simplify Meal Preparation**:
    - Offer finger foods or pre-cut items to make meals more manageable.
    - Serve meals in smaller portions to reduce overwhelm.
- **Promote Coordination**:
    - Practice with non-food items, like using tweezers to pick up cotton balls.
    - Engage in playful activities that build fine motor skills, such as stacking blocks.
- **Encourage Hydration**:
    - Use cups with lids and straws to prevent spills.
    - Offer insulated cups to maintain the desired temperature of drinks.
- **Support Positive Mealtime Experiences**:
    - Create a calm, distraction-free environment.
    - Use placemats or trays to help define personal space.

Organization and Time Management

Dyspraxia can affect executive functioning skills, making organization and time management a challenge. These strategies can help:

- **Visual Aids**:
    - Use visual schedules or timetables to outline daily routines.
    - Create color-coded calendars or to-do lists for easy reference.
- **Break Tasks into Steps**:
    - Divide complex activities into smaller, manageable parts.
    - Use checklists to track progress and encourage completion.
- **Establish Routines**:
    - Develop consistent morning and evening routines to build habits.
    - Use timers or alarms to help with transitions between tasks.
- **Designate Spaces for Essentials**:
    - Keep commonly used items like keys, shoes, and school supplies in dedicated spots.
    - Use labeled bins or drawers for easy access to belongings.
- **Incorporate Technology**:
    - Leverage apps for reminders, task management, or visual scheduling.
    - Use digital clocks with alarms set for key moments throughout the day.

- **Encourage Independence**:
    - Gradually increase your child's responsibility for planning their own day.
    - Provide gentle prompts as needed, focusing on their ability to complete tasks.

Sleep Routines

Establishing consistent sleep routines is essential for managing dyspraxia-related fatigue and improving overall well-being. Here are practical tips for better sleep:

- **Create a Consistent Schedule**:
    - Set regular bedtimes and wake-up times, even on weekends.
    - Use visual charts to outline bedtime routines.
- **Design a Sleep-Friendly Environment**:
    - Keep the bedroom cool, dark, and quiet.
    - Use blackout curtains or a white noise machine if necessary.
- **Limit Screen Time Before Bed**:
    - Avoid screens for at least an hour before bedtime to minimize blue light exposure.
    - Encourage relaxing activities like reading or listening to calming music.
- **Incorporate Relaxation Techniques**:
    - Teach deep breathing exercises or guided meditation to reduce anxiety.
    - Use weighted blankets or sensory-friendly bedding for comfort.
- **Address Sensory Needs**:
    - Provide pajamas that are soft and free of irritating tags or seams.

- Use nightlights or aromatherapy to create a soothing atmosphere.
- **Establish a Wind-Down Routine**:
  - Include calming activities like stretching, journaling, or storytelling.
  - Avoid stimulating activities like vigorous play or homework close to bedtime.

Encouragement and Support

Building daily living skills takes time and patience. Celebrate small victories and acknowledge progress along the way. Encourage your child to practice new tasks regularly, and don't hesitate to seek guidance from occupational therapists or other professionals when needed.

By implementing these strategies, you can help your child develop the confidence and skills they need to navigate daily life more independently.

Chapter 5: Supporting Motor Skills Development

Motor skills are foundational for many daily activities, from writing to playing sports. For children with dyspraxia, developing these skills can be challenging, but with targeted strategies and interventions, significant progress is achievable. This chapter explores fine motor activities, gross motor exercises, handwriting strategies, and the use of adaptive tools and technology.

Fine Motor Skills Activities

Fine motor skills involve small, precise movements, particularly those involving the hands and fingers. These skills are essential for tasks like writing, buttoning, and using utensils.

- **Play-Based Activities**:
    - **Craft Projects**: Engage in activities like bead stringing, finger painting, or cutting shapes with scissors.
    - **Puzzles and Manipulatives**: Use pegboards, puzzles, or toys like LEGO® to encourage hand coordination.
    - **Sensory Play**: Activities like molding clay or playing with sand provide tactile stimulation and strengthen hand muscles.
- **Everyday Tasks**:
    - Involve your child in practical tasks like sorting coins, tying shoelaces, or zipping up clothing.
    - Use kitchen activities like pouring liquids or stirring batter to practice coordination.
- **Therapy-Specific Exercises**:
    - Pinching exercises with clothespins to build finger strength.
    - Tracing shapes or letters to improve hand-eye coordination.

Gross Motor Skills Exercises

Gross motor skills involve larger body movements and coordination of the arms, legs, and trunk. Strengthening these skills enhances overall mobility and balance.

- **Core Stability and Balance**:
    - Activities like yoga or balancing on a wobble board can improve posture and core strength.
    - Practice simple balance exercises, such as standing on one foot or walking on a straight line.
- **Coordination Exercises**:
    - Play catch with balls of varying sizes to improve hand-eye coordination.
    - Engage in activities that involve crossing the midline, such as drawing large circles on a chalkboard or playing tug-of-war.
- **Structured Physical Activities**:
    - Encourage participation in swimming, which promotes full-body coordination.
    - Use obstacle courses with crawling, jumping, and climbing to develop spatial awareness and motor planning.

Handwriting Strategies

Handwriting can be particularly challenging for children with dyspraxia due to issues with grip, coordination, and spatial awareness. These strategies can help:

- **Improve Pencil Grip**:
    - Use pencil grips or ergonomic pens to encourage a proper grip.
    - Teach your child to hold the pencil with a tripod grasp.
- **Practice Letter Formation**:
    - Start with large movements, like forming letters in the air or tracing them in sand, before progressing to paper.
    - Use lined or graph paper to help with letter alignment and spacing.
- **Break Down Tasks**:
    - Focus on one letter or word at a time, providing clear, step-by-step guidance.
    - Encourage frequent breaks to prevent fatigue and frustration.
- **Incorporate Visual and Tactile Cues**:
    - Use stencils or raised-line paper to guide handwriting.
    - Add verbal prompts, like "start at the top" or "make a circle," to reinforce direction.

Using Adaptive Tools and Technology

Adaptive tools and technology can significantly enhance motor skills development by providing support and reducing frustration.

- **Fine Motor Aids**:
    - Adaptive scissors with spring assistance can make cutting easier.
    - Weighted utensils or tools help improve control and reduce tremors.

- **Assistive Writing Tools**:
  - Try slanted writing boards to position the paper for easier access.
  - Use mechanical pencils with soft grips to reduce hand strain.
- **Technology for Motor Skills**:
  - **Tablets and Apps**: Apps designed for children with motor difficulties can provide engaging ways to practice skills, such as tracing or drawing games.
  - **Speech-to-Text Software**: Reduces reliance on handwriting while enabling effective communication.
  - **Interactive Whiteboards**: Promote whole-body movements while working on writing and drawing.
- **Virtual Reality and Games**:
  - Incorporate technology-based interventions like virtual reality games or serious games specifically designed for motor training.
  - Activities in virtual environments can enhance coordination and simulate real-world tasks in a fun, low-pressure way.

Task-Oriented Approaches

Recent research highlights the effectiveness of task-oriented interventions, such as the **Cognitive Orientation to Daily Occupational Performance (CO-OP)** approach. This method focuses on teaching children to:

- Break tasks into smaller, manageable steps.
- Use verbal self-guidance to direct their actions.
- Evaluate and adjust their strategies to achieve success.

For example, a child learning to tie their shoelaces might use a step-by-step verbal sequence: "Cross the laces, make a loop, pull through."

Encouragement and Patience

Motor skills development takes time, especially for children with dyspraxia. Celebrate small achievements and provide consistent encouragement. Regular practice, combined with the right tools and strategies, will build your child's confidence and independence.

Chapter 6: Enhancing Learning and Academic Performance

Children with dyspraxia often face unique challenges in academic settings. However, with the right strategies and support, they can thrive in school and build confidence in their abilities. This chapter focuses on working with the school to implement accommodations, homework strategies, and tailored approaches to support reading, writing, math, and problem-solving skills.

Working with the School to Implement Accommodations

Collaborating with your child's school is essential to create an environment that supports their learning needs. Here's how to ensure effective accommodations:

- **Develop an Individualized Plan**:
    - Work with the school to create an Individualized Education Plan (IEP) or a 504 Plan, which outlines specific accommodations and goals.
    - Ensure the plan is regularly reviewed and updated to reflect your child's progress.
- **Focus on Classroom Modifications**:
    - Seating arrangements: Place your child near the teacher or away from distractions.
    - Simplify instructions: Provide clear, concise, and step-by-step directions.
    - Visual aids: Use charts, diagrams, and other visual tools to reinforce concepts.
- **Advocate for Assistive Technology**:
    - Tools like text-to-speech software, word prediction programs, or digital organizers can help bridge gaps in learning.
    - Encourage the use of tablets or laptops for writing tasks to reduce the strain of handwriting.
- **Promote Teacher Training**:
    - Share resources about dyspraxia with educators to help them understand your child's needs.

- o Suggest professional development workshops focused on supporting children with motor and coordination challenges.
- **Build Regular Communication**:
  - o Set up periodic meetings with teachers to discuss progress and challenges.
  - o Use a communication notebook or email updates to stay informed about your child's day-to-day experiences.

Homework Strategies

Homework can be overwhelming for children with dyspraxia, but structured approaches can make it more manageable:

- **Create a Dedicated Workspace**:
  - o Set up a quiet, clutter-free area for homework.
  - o Provide necessary tools, such as pencils with grips, graph paper, and a timer.
- **Break Tasks Into Smaller Steps**:
  - o Divide assignments into manageable sections, focusing on one part at a time.
  - o Use checklists to track completed tasks and provide a sense of accomplishment.
- **Establish a Routine**:
  - o Set a consistent time each day for homework to build a predictable habit.
  - o Include short breaks to maintain focus and reduce frustration.
- **Use Visual Schedules**:
  - o Create a timeline with start and end times for each task.

- o Incorporate visual cues, like colored markers or stickers, to indicate progress.
- **Provide Support and Encouragement**:
  - o Offer gentle guidance and reassurance, avoiding criticism if your child struggles.
  - o Celebrate small achievements to build confidence and motivation.

Reading and Writing Support

Reading and writing may pose challenges due to coordination and processing difficulties. Tailored strategies can enhance these skills:

- **Reading Support**:
  - o Use audiobooks or paired reading to reduce the stress of decoding text.
  - o Highlight keywords in assignments to help your child focus on essential information.
  - o Encourage the use of rulers or reading guides to track lines of text.
- **Writing Support**:
  - o Provide templates or sentence starters to help structure writing tasks.
  - o Teach keyboarding skills early to offer an alternative to handwriting.
  - o Use adaptive tools, such as pencil grips, slant boards, or speech-to-text software.
- **Encourage Creative Expression**:
  - o Allow your child to dictate stories or ideas for you to write or type.
  - o Use graphic organizers or mind maps to brainstorm and organize thoughts.

Math and Problem-Solving Techniques

Dyspraxia can affect spatial awareness, sequencing, and memory, which are critical for math. These strategies can help:

- **Use Hands-On Tools**:
  - Manipulatives like counting blocks, number lines, or fraction circles make abstract concepts tangible.
  - Apps and interactive games designed for math can reinforce learning in an engaging way.
- **Simplify Instructions**:
  - Break math problems into smaller, clear steps with examples.
  - Provide written instructions alongside verbal explanations.
- **Focus on Visual Learning**:
  - Use diagrams, charts, or color-coded methods to represent data.
  - Encourage your child to draw pictures or models to solve word problems.
- **Practice Mental Math Gradually**:
  - Start with simple calculations and gradually increase complexity.
  - Use repetition and practice to build confidence and fluency.
- **Provide Timed Practice**:
  - Encourage timed activities to improve speed and focus, but keep the goals realistic.

- Use timers or gamified apps to make practice fun and motivating.

Incorporating Technology in Learning

Technology can be a game-changer for children with dyspraxia, offering tools to overcome specific challenges:

- **Reading Apps**: Use apps with features like text highlighting and audio playback to aid comprehension.
- **Math Tools**: Interactive software like Mathletics or KhanAcademy can break down complex concepts.
- **Organization Apps**: Digital calendars, task managers, and visual schedule apps help with time management.

Encouragement and Support

Academic success isn't just about grades—it's about building confidence, resilience, and a love of learning. With the right strategies and a strong support system, your child can overcome challenges and achieve their full potential.

Chapter 7: Nurturing Social Skills and Emoãonal Well-Being

Children with dyspraxia often face challenges in social settings and may struggle with emotional regulation. By fostering self-esteem, promoting friendships, and teaching coping strategies, parents can help their children build resilience and navigate the complexities of social and emotional life. This chapter focuses on building confidence, developing friendships, managing anxiety and frustration, and encouraging independence.

Building Self-Esteem and Confidence

Self-esteem is the foundation of emotional well-being and social success. Children with dyspraxia may face setbacks that affect their confidence, but small, consistent efforts can help them feel valued and capable.

- **Focus on Strengths**:
    - Highlight your child's unique talents and interests, such as creativity, problem-solving, or a love for music or art.
    - Celebrate small achievements and milestones, no matter how minor they may seem.
- **Set Achievable Goals**:
    - Help your child set realistic, short-term goals they can accomplish.
    - Break larger tasks into smaller steps to make success more attainable.
- **Provide Encouragement**:
    - Use positive reinforcement to motivate your child.
    - Avoid overly critical language and instead focus on solutions and progress.
- **Promote Participation**:
    - Encourage your child to engage in activities where they can shine, such as art classes, music lessons, or coding workshops.
    - Allow them to explore hobbies that align with their strengths and interests.

Developing Friendships

Building friendships can be challenging for children with dyspraxia due to difficulties with coordination, communication, or understanding social cues. These strategies can help your child form meaningful connections:

- **Model Social Skills**:
  - Role-play common social interactions, such as introducing oneself or asking to join a group activity.
  - Teach them to read body language, facial expressions, and tone of voice.
- **Facilitate Opportunities**:
  - Arrange playdates or small group activities with peers who share similar interests.
  - Encourage participation in clubs or extracurricular activities to meet like-minded children.
- **Teach Empathy and Communication**:
  - Practice active listening skills with your child, such as maintaining eye contact and asking follow-up questions.
  - Emphasize the importance of kindness and respect in friendships.
- **Support Peer Relationships**:
  - Help your child navigate conflicts by teaching problem-solving strategies.
  - Celebrate their friendships and encourage efforts to maintain them.

Managing Anxiety and Frustration

Children with dyspraxia may feel overwhelmed by daily challenges, leading to anxiety or frustration. Teaching them to manage these emotions can improve their well-being and interactions.

- **Identify Triggers**:
    - Observe and document situations that cause anxiety or frustration, such as new environments or difficult tasks.
    - Work with your child to anticipate and prepare for these situations.
- **Teach Coping Strategies**:
    - Practice deep breathing exercises or mindfulness techniques to help them calm down.
    - Encourage the use of sensory tools, such as stress balls or fidget toys, to manage tension.
- **Create a Safe Space**:
    - Establish a quiet area at home where your child can retreat when feeling overwhelmed.
    - Use calming visuals, sounds, or scents to create a soothing atmosphere.
- **Build Emotional Vocabulary**:
    - Help your child express their feelings by teaching them words to describe emotions.
    - Use tools like emotion charts or journals to encourage self-reflection.

Encouraging Independence

Fostering independence helps children with dyspraxia feel empowered and capable of navigating their world.

- **Start Small**:
    - Assign age-appropriate responsibilities, such as packing their school bag or setting the table.

- o Provide step-by-step instructions and gradually reduce assistance.
- **Encourage Problem-Solving**:
  - o Allow your child to make choices and solve simple problems on their own.
  - o Offer guidance only when necessary to build their confidence in decision-making.
- **Promote Self-Advocacy**:
  - o Teach your child to communicate their needs to teachers, peers, and others.
  - o Role-play scenarios where they may need to ask for help or explain their challenges.
- **Celebrate Independence**:
  - o Acknowledge and reward their efforts to complete tasks on their own.
  - o Use positive reinforcement to encourage continued growth.

Supporting Holistic Well-Being

Fostering social skills and emotional resilience is a journey that requires patience and consistency. By building your child's confidence, encouraging friendships, teaching coping strategies, and supporting their independence, you can help them thrive socially and emotionally.

Chapter 8: Physical Activities and Sports

Physical activities and sports provide valuable opportunities for children with dyspraxia to develop strength, coordination, and confidence. However, traditional sports may need to be adapted to suit their needs. This chapter explores how to choose appropriate activities, adapt sports and games, build motor skills, and celebrate effort and progress.

Choosing Appropriate Activities

Selecting the right physical activities is essential to ensure your child feels engaged, supported, and successful.

- **Focus on Enjoyment:**
    - Prioritize activities your child enjoys rather than those deemed "traditional" or popular.

- Experiment with various options to discover their preferences.

- **Encourage Non-Competitive Sports**:
  - Opt for activities like swimming, martial arts, or yoga, which focus on individual progress rather than team competition.
  - Consider creative movement classes, such as dance, which allow self-expression.
- **Match Activities to Abilities**:
  - Look for sports or games that align with your child's current motor skills and strengths.
  - Avoid high-pressure environments where coordination difficulties might be a barrier.
- **Explore Sensory-Friendly Options**:
  - Activities like water play, cycling, or trampoline exercises can provide sensory input while building motor skills.

Adapting Sports and Games

Adapting sports can make them more inclusive and enjoyable for children with dyspraxia.

- **Modify Rules**:
  - Simplify game rules to reduce complexity and increase understanding.
  - Allow extra time for tasks, such as catching or throwing, to accommodate motor challenges.

- **Adapt Equipment**:
    - Use lighter balls, larger rackets, or other modified equipment for easier handling.
    - Choose brightly colored or textured items for improved visibility and grip.
- **Create a Supportive Environment**:
    - Foster a team culture that emphasizes participation and fun over competition.
    - Pair your child with a buddy or mentor who can guide and encourage them during activities.
- **Break Activities Into Steps**:
    - Teach skills like kicking or throwing in small, manageable steps with clear instructions.
    - Provide frequent practice opportunities to reinforce learning.

Building Strength and Coordination

Strength and coordination are key to improving physical abilities and overcoming dyspraxia-related challenges.

- **Strengthening Exercises**:
    - Use resistance bands or body-weight exercises to build muscle tone.
    - Incorporate activities like climbing or pulling, which engage multiple muscle groups.
- **Balance and Coordination Drills**:
    - Practice activities that challenge balance, such as standing on one foot or using a balance board.
    - Encourage games like hopscotch or obstacle courses to improve spatial awareness.

- **Hand-Eye Coordination Games**:
  - Try activities like tossing beanbags into a target or hitting a balloon with a paddle.
  - Use video games designed for motor skill development as a fun alternative.
- **Structured Physical Therapy**:
  - Work with an occupational or physical therapist to design a tailored exercise plan.
  - Focus on specific goals, such as improving gait, posture, or fine motor coordination.

Celebrating Effort and Progress

Recognizing and rewarding effort can help your child build confidence and maintain motivation.

- **Focus on Personal Growth**:
  - Celebrate improvements, no matter how small, such as kicking a ball farther or maintaining balance for longer.
  - Avoid comparisons to peers; instead, highlight their unique progress.
- **Use Positive Reinforcement**:
  - Offer praise or small rewards for participation and effort, not just outcomes.
  - Use phrases like "I'm proud of how hard you worked!" to emphasize their determination.
- **Encourage Perseverance**:
  - Teach your child that mistakes and setbacks are part of the learning process.
  - Share stories of athletes or individuals who overcame challenges to inspire resilience.

- **Document Achievements**:
  - Keep a journal, chart, or photo album to track milestones and accomplishments.
  - Reflect on progress over time to boost morale and motivation.

Promoting Inclusion in Sports

Advocating for inclusion in community sports programs can create opportunities for your child to engage and thrive:

- Encourage local sports leagues to offer adaptive programs.
- Educate coaches and peers about dyspraxia to foster understanding and support.

By choosing the right activities, adapting sports to fit your child's needs, and focusing on effort and progress, you can help them develop physical skills, build confidence, and enjoy the many benefits of staying active.

Chapter 9: Planning for the Future

Planning for the future is a crucial step in supporting children with dyspraxia as they transition through different stages of life. From secondary school to adulthood, fostering independence, career readiness, and a positive outlook can set the stage for lifelong success. This chapter covers transitioning to secondary school, career planning and vocational support, building life skills for independence, and long-term outlooks with inspiring success stories.

Transitioning to Secondary School

The move to secondary school marks a significant milestone in a child's education. For children with dyspraxia, preparation and support are key to a smooth transition.

- **Prepare Early**:
    - Visit the school with your child to familiarize them with the layout and routine.
    - Meet with teachers, learning support staff, and counselors to discuss your child's needs.
- **Develop Organizational Skills**:
    - Use color-coded folders or labeled binders for each subject.
    - Encourage the use of planners or digital tools to track assignments and deadlines.
- **Accommodations and Support**:
    - Work with the school to create an updated Individualized Education Plan (IEP) or equivalent.
    - Request accommodations such as extra time for exams, assistive technology, or alternative PE activities.
- **Encourage Self-Advocacy**:
    - Teach your child to communicate their needs to teachers and peers.
    - Role-play scenarios, such as asking for help or explaining dyspraxia, to build confidence.

Career Planning and Vocational Support

As children with dyspraxia approach adolescence, exploring career options and vocational skills becomes increasingly important.

- **Identify Strengths and Interests**:
    - Help your child discover their passions and abilities through hobbies, extracurricular activities, or internships.
    - Focus on careers that align with their strengths, such as creativity, problem-solving, or empathy.
- **Develop Workplace Skills**:
    - Practice professional skills like time management, teamwork, and communication.
    - Use real-life experiences, such as volunteering or part-time jobs, to build confidence.
- **Leverage Vocational Support**:
    - Seek out programs that provide career counseling and job placement services for individuals with learning or motor challenges.
    - Explore internships or apprenticeships to offer hands-on experience in their fields of interest.
- **Teach Digital Literacy**:
    - Equip your child with skills in using technology and software relevant to their career goals.

- Encourage familiarity with adaptive tools that can enhance workplace productivity.

Life Skills for Independence

Building life skills is essential for fostering independence and preparing for adulthood. Focus on practical, everyday abilities:

- **Financial Literacy**:
  - Teach your child to manage a budget, save money, and understand basic banking tasks.
  - Use tools like budgeting apps to simplify financial management.
- **Household Management**:
  - Involve your child in chores like cooking, cleaning, and laundry to build confidence in handling domestic tasks.
  - Break tasks into smaller steps and provide visual or written guides for reference.
- **Social and Interpersonal Skills**:
  - Practice social etiquette, such as making introductions, maintaining eye contact, and active listening.
  - Encourage participation in community events or social groups to build relationships.
- **Transportation Skills**:
  - Teach your child how to navigate public transportation systems or learn to drive if appropriate.
  - Role-play scenarios like purchasing tickets or asking for directions.

- **Health and Wellness**:
  - Encourage your child to manage their health by scheduling appointments, understanding medications, and adopting healthy habits.
  - Provide guidance on preparing balanced meals and maintaining regular exercise routines.

Long-Term Outlook and Success Stories

A positive outlook is crucial for envisioning a fulfilling and successful future. Share examples of individuals with dyspraxia who have achieved their goals.

- **Highlight Achievements**:
  - Share stories of adults with dyspraxia who have excelled in various fields, from the arts to technology.
  - Discuss the unique qualities that helped them succeed, such as creativity, resilience, or empathy.
- **Celebrate Progress**:
  - Reflect on your child's journey and the milestones they've achieved along the way.
  - Emphasize that success is not defined by societal norms but by personal growth and fulfillment.
- **Focus on Ongoing Support**:
  - Recognize that challenges may persist, but with the right resources and mindset, they can be managed effectively.
  - Encourage lifelong learning and adaptability to navigate future changes.

Empowering the Journey Ahead

Planning for the future is about equipping children with dyspraxia with the tools, confidence, and resilience they need to thrive. By supporting their transitions, fostering independence, and highlighting success stories, you can help them envision a bright and fulfilling future.

Chapter 10: Self-Care for Parents

Caring for a child with dyspraxia is rewarding but can also be physically and emotionally demanding. Prioritizing your well-being is not selfish—it's essential for maintaining the strength and resilience needed to support your child. This chapter explores strategies for managing stress, finding personal time, maintaining a balanced family life, and seeking support.

Managing Stress and Emotions

Parenting a child with dyspraxia often comes with unique challenges that can lead to stress and emotional strain. Here are ways to cope effectively:

- **Acknowledge Your Feelings**:
  - Accept that it's okay to feel overwhelmed, frustrated, or uncertain at times.
  - Journaling your thoughts or speaking with a trusted friend can help you process emotions.
- **Practice Stress-Reduction Techniques**:
  - Incorporate mindfulness or meditation into your daily routine to center yourself.
  - Engage in physical activities like yoga, walking, or swimming to release tension.

- **Set Realistic Expectations**:
  - Avoid striving for perfection—focus on doing your best, one day at a time.
  - Recognize and celebrate small victories, both for yourself and your child.
- **Avoid Burnout**:
  - Monitor your energy levels and take breaks when needed.
  - Delegate tasks to your partner, family members, or trusted friends.

Finding Time for Yourself

Making time for yourself can feel impossible when caring for a child with special needs, but even small moments of self-care can rejuvenate you.

- **Schedule "Me Time"**:
  - Set aside at least 15–30 minutes each day to do something you enjoy, such as reading, gardening, or listening to music.
  - Treat this time as non-negotiable and plan it into your daily routine.
- **Pursue Hobbies and Interests**:
  - Reconnect with activities you love, whether it's painting, baking, or attending fitness classes.
  - Join clubs or groups that align with your interests to meet like-minded individuals.
- **Practice Saying No**:
  - Learn to decline additional responsibilities or commitments that may overwhelm you.
  - Focus your energy on what truly matters for your well-being and family.

- **Utilize Support Systems**:
  - Enlist the help of family, friends, or babysitters to give yourself a well-deserved break.
  - Consider respite care services for longer periods of rest or rejuvenation.

Maintaining a Balanced Family Life

Creating harmony within the family ensures that everyone's needs are met, fostering a supportive and nurturing environment.

- **Prioritize Communication**:
  - Hold regular family meetings to discuss schedules, challenges, and achievements.
  - Encourage open dialogue, where every family member can share their feelings and ideas.
- **Strengthen Relationships**:
  - Dedicate quality time to your partner, whether it's a date night or a quiet evening at home.
  - Spend one-on-one time with each child to ensure they feel valued and connected.
- **Establish Family Routines**:
  - Consistent routines for meals, bedtime, and activities help reduce stress for everyone.
  - Involve your children in planning family activities to promote teamwork and inclusion.

- **Celebrate Together**:
    - Acknowledge milestones and accomplishments as a family.
    - Create traditions or rituals, such as family game nights or outings, to build joyful memories.

Seeking Support When Needed

Knowing when to ask for help is a sign of strength, not weakness. A robust support network can make all the difference.

- **Join Support Groups**:
    - Connect with other parents of children with dyspraxia to share experiences, advice, and encouragement.
    - Online forums and local support meetings can provide valuable resources and emotional validation.
- **Seek Professional Help**:
    - Consult therapists or counselors for individual or family sessions to address stress and emotional challenges.
    - Consider workshops or training programs that equip you with parenting tools and strategies.
- **Access Community Resources**:
    - Explore services offered by local organizations, such as childcare, respite care, or financial assistance programs.
    - Attend seminars or conferences on dyspraxia to stay informed and empowered.

- **Involve Extended Family and Friends:**
    - Educate loved ones about dyspraxia and how they can support your family.
    - Don't hesitate to delegate tasks or accept help when it's offered.

Taking Care of Yourself Benefits Everyone

By prioritizing your self-care, you set a powerful example for your child and family. A well-rested, emotionally balanced parent is better equipped to handle challenges, celebrate successes, and create a loving and stable home environment.

Conclusion

The journey of raising a child with dyspraxia is one of resilience, adaptation, and celebration. By understanding the condition, building a strong support network, and implementing practical strategies, you can empower your child to navigate challenges and embrace their unique potential. This conclusion recaps key takeaways, offers words of encouragement, and provides resources for ongoing support.

Recap of Key Points

1. **Understanding Dyspraxia**:
    - Dyspraxia is a neurodevelopmental condition affecting motor coordination and planning, requiring tailored interventions for success.
2. **Building Support Networks**:
    - Collaborate with healthcare professionals, educators, and support groups to create a comprehensive framework of assistance.
3. **Practical Strategies**:
    - Implement targeted activities to improve motor skills, academic performance, and social-emotional well-being.
    - Use adaptive tools and technology to bridge gaps and enhance learning.
4. **Fostering Independence**:
    - Teach life skills, promote self-advocacy, and prepare your child for transitions to secondary school, careers, and adulthood.
5. **Parent Self-Care**:
    - Prioritize your well-being to sustain the energy and emotional resilience needed to support your child.

Words of Encouragement

Remember, progress is not linear, and setbacks are part of growth. Celebrate every milestone, no matter how small, and take pride in the strength and perseverance of your family. Your child's challenges are only one aspect of who they are—they have incredible potential, talents, and the ability to succeed on their terms. Trust in your efforts, seek support when needed, and know that you're not alone in this journey.

Resources for Further Information and Support

The following resources can provide valuable information, tools, and connections to help you continue advocating for your child:

- National and international dyspraxia organizations.
- Online forums and support groups.
- Local community services and workshops.

Appendices

The appendices offer additional tools and resources to support your journey as a parent of a child with dyspraxia.

Glossary of Terms

A quick reference for key terms related to dyspraxia and its management:

- **Dyspraxia**: A developmental coordination disorder affecting motor skills and planning.
- **IEP (Individualized Education Plan)**: A personalized learning plan for children with special educational needs.
- **Occupational Therapy**: Therapy focusing on improving fine motor skills and daily living tasks.
- **CO-OP (Cognitive Orientation to Daily Occupational Performance)**: A task-oriented intervention approach.

Checklists and Worksheets

Use these practical tools to stay organized and support your child's development:

- **Daily Routine Checklist**: A visual guide to help your child follow daily schedules.
- **Task Breakdown Worksheet**: Step-by-step guides for completing complex activities.
- **IEP Meeting Prep Checklist**: A list of key documents and questions for school meetings.

Recommended Reading List

Explore these books and articles for deeper insights into dyspraxia:
- Articles and journals on motor skills development
- *Raising a Child with Dyspraxia* by Amanda Kirby
- *The Out-of-Sync Child* by Carol Kranowitz
  and educational strategies.

Directory of Organizations and Support Groups

Connect with these organizations for guidance, resources, and community support:

- **Dyspraxia Foundation**: A leading source of information, webinars, and local support groups.
- **Local Educational Agencies**: Contact your regional office for special education resources.
- **Online Communities**:
    - Facebook groups or Reddit forums focused on dyspraxia.
    - National Autism Society websites that also cover co-occurring conditions like dyspraxia.

Looking Ahead

The tools, strategies, and resources shared in this book are designed to support you in raising a confident, independent, and thriving child. Trust in your abilities as a parent and remember that every step forward—no matter how small—is a victory worth celebrating.

Read More Books Written by Jagdish Prasad Yadav

www.ingramcontent.com/pod-product-compliance
Lightning Source LLC
Chambersburg PA
CBHW072106110526
44590CB00018B/3335